THE MUSIC WAS THE THING

Zara Jones

CAVERN CITY TOURS LIMITED
LIVERPOOL

Acknowledgements

First and foremost I would like to thank all the people who participated in the project. They had nothing to gain from doing so – no fees or press exposure, just a genuine love of "fab" music. I would also like to thank all the people who arranged photo/interview sessions for me, Bill Heckle, Dave Jones and all at Cavern City Tours for not only allowing me access to The Cavern Club's celebrity guests, but for making this book a reality, Chas Cole (CMP) for helping me build the foundation of the project at Summer Pops 2001/2002, Peter Grant (Liverpool Echo) for writing a piece on the project, suggesting the cover concept and inspiring me to use props other than LP covers, Mark Jones (BitBiz), Les 'Speedy Gonzales' Davies (NPS) and last, but not least, CD Petee for rescuing the Adele photo. Rest in peace Victor Spinetti, Robert Whitaker and Gary Moore (Lord of The Strings).

You may be interested to know that the following photos were taken in Liverpool's famous Cavern Club, where The Beatles played 292 times:
Steve Adler (page 9)
Stan Boardman (page 27)
Ken Dodd (page 35)
Richie Havens (page 55)
Chas and Dave (page 93)
Adele (page 121).

All photographs and interviews are copyright of Zara Jones/3rd Person Photography 2012. Where two dates appear beside an entry, the first represents the year of the interview and the second refers to the year that the photograph was taken.

Please join me on Facebook:
facebook.com/3rdpersonphotos
facebook.com/themusicwasthething

Published by Cavern City Tours Ltd.
The Cavern Club, 10 Mathew Street, Liverpool L2 6RE

Typeset by NPS Phototypesetting
Printed by Print On Demand, Peterborough
© Zara Jones/3rd Person Photography 2012
First published in Great Britain in 2012
ISBN 978-1-873111-02-4

Introduction

My first memory of The Beatles is listening to *Rubber Soul* (still my favourite album) whilst working through a dot-to-dot book on a rainy day. I would have been about four. I was certain that the album cover featured the same man four times, and that the picture of John (on the back cover) was taken in the 'Norwegian wood'. Beatles songs have always had a special kind of magic to me – their melodies and lyrics have always conjured up images in my mind, usually pleasant ones, although *Run For Your Life* and *Eleanor Rigby* both terrified me back then.

In 1995, I watched The Beatles Anthology TV series and my respect and fascination for the Fab Four grew even further. Until that point I hadn't realised that songs I knew from playground chants (*Yellow Submarine*) and charity cover versions (*Help!*, *Let It Be*) were written by the same men who'd created the wonderful *Rubber Soul* album I'd loved for all those years. I eagerly watched the footage of them being chased by hysterical fans, joking and philosophising in interviews and finding spiritual enlightenment in India. As their hair grew longer, the world literally changed from black and white to colour. It completely amazed me. I began to correspond with other young Beatles fans through pen pal adverts in music magazines. There were other people who understood, I was no longer a misfit.

In 1999, I embarked upon the first incarnation of this project. I asked my new found friends to pose with a Beatles album of their choice, which then became a public request. I took pictures of shop assistants, bus drivers, car-park attendants, even asking strangers to send in contributions via an advert in the Beatles Book Monthly. The idea was not only to pay tribute to The Beatles' influence and legacy, but to show that, just as each album varies from the last, so too do the people who listen to them. Not so much are you a Taurus or a Leo, but are you a *Sergeant Pepper* or a *With The Beatles*?

The following year I photographed Klaus Voormann with the album he designed the cover for, *Revolver*, technically making him the first participant in this book (although I didn't get to interview him until several years later). From there, I decided to try and contact both celebrity Beatles fans, and those who aren't necessarily famous, but whose music or art inspires me. It also struck me to try and find out why people had chosen a particular album – not just a list of their favourite songs, but the memories and feelings evoked from listening to them. The music was the thing, yes, but the music was also the soundtrack to some unique and special moments in people's lives.

The first few photos were captured by taking a single shaky shot on my cheap compact film camera. As the years passed, my camera equipment and confidence gradually improved, although the finished product was never going to be an exercise in fine art photography. There was never any glitz, glamour or studio lighting, just a few snatched moments where and whenever I could grab them. Some images are very raw and basic, others are more polished and creative (you might say the same of the recordings they are paying tribute to); however, each one is genuine. No albums were 'added later'.

For the most part, I found it very hard trying to convince mangers and PR people of my idea. In the words of former press photographer Stephen Shakeshaft: "I've learnt that it's not the stars who don't want to be photographed or talk to the press, but the bureaucrats around them." Thankfully there are exceptions to this, or the book would never have been finished. Sometimes many months would pass without success, but I was determined not to give up until my mission was complete.

"Tell them the music was the thing."
(John Lennon's message to a 1970's Beatles convention)

❛I don't necessarily think that *Please Please Me* is The Beatles' best album, but I do think that it is their most significant. It started the revolution, it kicked open the door worldwide. I think I was a bit too close to it all to see the importance of The Beatles at the time. I just viewed them as people from the Liverpool scene who had done well for themselves. When Paul gave me a copy of the *Help!* album, I never for one moment thought about getting it signed. It was just a gift from a friend. The significance of it all has grown over time.❜

JOHN GORMAN (The Scaffold) - 2008

❮I remember hearing *Love Me Do* and it didn't really make that much of an impression on me. I liked it, but it was nothing like the impression that their albums and the later singles made on me. When we heard their first album, it changed our lives completely. That's all we listened to, and it influenced us incredibly. We used to open our act with *I Saw Her Standing There* and we probably covered at least half of the album – *Misery, Love Me Do, Twist And Shout*. Before The Beatles came along, I think that people believed that musicians who played live and songwriters were two completely different crafts. You weren't expected to write songs; in fact, I think you were almost discouraged from writing songs if you were an artiste, and it probably worked the other way round as well. The Beatles did change everything, and maybe that's part of the reason why Rod Argent and Chris White started writing. I remember that our producer said: "We've got a studio date booked in a couple of weeks, why don't you try and write something?" And possibly, if they hadn't heard The Beatles, they wouldn't have had the confidence to go away and try. Rod went on to write *She's Not There*, which sold a million copies!

Vocally, it would always be Paul McCartney for me. When he sings a rock 'n' roll song he's got great range, great phrasing. *Back In The USSR* is one of my favourites. It's such a wonderful, unusual lyric. It's so hard to write something like that, and I think it's a very musical song as well. I thought a lot of the McCartney songs were very musical, they're not the kind of songs that would be your first songs. When you first start writing it's usually an introverted four-chord love song, but a lot of the songs that he wrote sound really sophisticated. How did he write that? How *did* he write that? He's just fantastic. I think everything starts with songwriting. I always say that if you haven't got a really good song, you can all pack up and go home! Lennon and McCartney are two of the most prolific and brilliant songwriters that have ever been, but there were other things as well – they played great as a band and were recorded very well. We were the next band into Abbey Road studios after they'd done *Sergeant Pepper* and we used some of the same engineers for *Odessey And Oracle*. Geoff Emerick in particular, who recorded a lot of their albums, and also Peter Vince. During *Pepper*, they'd made a lot of changes to recording technique and improvised things in the studio that had never been done before. We were one of the first groups to benefit from those improvisations.❯

COLIN BLUNSTONE (The Zombies) - 2011

❛My mother made me aware of The Beatles when I was around five years old. I love the energy of this album, songs like *I Saw Her Standing There*, but also the ballads like *Do You Want To Know A Secret?* All of it is pure magic. I think they were the first bunch of guys, young rebellious guys, who used their image to create music, not to go round fighting or looking tough. I mean you've got to look at their hair on this cover – that was long hair back then! Sure, people like Little Richard had been rebellious before, but this was a gang for the first time. They created a magic that's not possible to create unless you have that closeness with the other band members. I remember that when Slash and I were playing together for the first time, the only song we could both gel tightly with was *Day Tripper*. And John Lennon – well, he was a cool motherfucker!❜

STEVE ADLER (Guns N' Roses) – 2006

❝I was a raw, young trainee at Granada TV in Manchester, and one of my earliest assignments for their regional magazine programme, *People and Places*, was to organise a series of short films. The brief was to find subjects which would illustrate the contrasts between tradition and innovation in our region. One of the subjects was music. We filmed first with the Brighouse and Rastrick Brass Band to represent the traditional angle, then I looked around for the most contrasting music in our area. I heard about some kids who were playing rock 'n' roll in a Liverpool cellar. Though they had fans around Liverpool, they hadn't yet released any records. I was told to contact a man called Brian Epstein, and found myself meeting an unlikely rock manager – an elegant man in a three-piece suit. Epstein led me down the stone steps into The Cavern Club and I got my first taste of The Beatles. I was, and still am, a modern jazz fan, but the music flooding up those stairs was instantly thrilling, stirring my guts. Joining the sweating kids jammed into The Cavern, I was grabbed by the sheer power and vitality of the music roaring out of the embryonic fab four. I was hooked. I guess I had been expecting something like Cliff and The Shadows. Remember, this was 1962 and there was nothing to prepare me for the impact of The Beatles. They were playing searing versions of American R&B classics – *Mr Postman, Money, Some Other Guy, Roll Over Beethoven*. There was no evidence of their own songs. I went backstage to meet the boys. I remember Lennon wringing out his sweat-soaked shirt into a bucket. They were fun and friendly, especially the one with the implacable charm of a spaniel, Paul McCartney. He said to me: "It must be dead glamorous being in TV". I thought the one called John looked less impressed. They said they'd written lots of songs, but nobody wanted to hear them. I said I'd come back and film them in a few days. And so, on August 22nd 1962, I found myself shooting the first ever film with The Beatles. I chose *Some Other Guy*, and they also did *Kansas City*. I recall being surrounded by kids yelling "we want Pete" and being told this was a first gig for a new drummer, Ringo Starr.

I bought *With The Beatles* in Manchester as soon as it was released. I loved it because it sounded like the group I followed around the northern clubs after our filming. I enjoyed the old Cavern favourites on the album: *Roll Over Beethoven, Mr Postman*, and *Money*, and, of course, there's the classic *All My Loving*, with a celebrated George Harrison country and western style solo. George also had his first chance as a composer with *Don't Bother Me*, including Ringo on an Arabian bongo! My favourite track is the opening number, *It Won't Be Long*. It roars away with John's searing vocal, and I always loved the repeating bass riff which powers through the song. I thought the album's cover, with its ultra-stylish Bob Freeman photo, looked as cool as my cherished modern jazz albums. I also had a special connection with the album because, at that time, The Beatles came regularly to the Granada studios to perform their latest hits, and I used to go and say hi.

What's remarkable about The Beatles is how consistently surprising, fresh and inventive their albums are, and how rapidly their music develops and evolves. Inevitably, on some albums there are tracks I can live without; some of George's Indian things, John's wilder experiments, or Paul's cuter songs. Like many people, I'm unhappy with Phil Spector's overblown intrusions on *Let it Be*, but for me, there are no dud albums. Having recently made my BBC film, *How The Beatles Rocked The Kremlin*, I'm also fascinated by The Beatles' impact in the former Soviet Union. They were never able to play there, and it was illegal to have one of their albums, but millions of people found their way to Beatles music. Many told me it changed their lives. They said they found freedom and release in the music, and it prepared them for change and the overthrow of totalitarianism. Some people even told me they'd seen that little film I made in The Cavern, long ago. The fundamental secret of their longevity, I think, is that their blend of talents made them unique, and for all time. Also, there was some genius in the mix. Between them, they wrote songs that will live on as long as people enjoy melody.❞

LESLIE WOODHEAD (Documentary film-maker) - 2009

'My sister Marg used to go and watch live music at The Cavern. Ringo once asked her to dance, although he was still with Rory Storm and the Hurricanes at the time. She saw The Beatles when they were just newcomers at the club and would talk about John being really funny on stage. My own enthusiasm for them began around 1963. I would probably have been aware of their first album, *Please Please Me*, but *With The Beatles* was where my interest began. We had a radiogram at home which usually played records by Tony Bennett and Frank Sinatra, but as soon as we had a copy of *With The Beatles*, it would be on there constantly. I loved the LP cover, the way that they had been photographed in black and white – half light and half shade, similar to the way that Astrid Kirchherr had photographed them previously. Every week I would go skating at Silver Blades ice rink, where they would always play *Till There Was You*. I loved it. The original version of the song had featured in a musical, and the entertainment industry was something I was already very interested in. The person I most admired was Jimmy Tarbuck, who appeared on *Sunday Night at the London Palladium*. Jimmy was like the fifth Beatle. He would speak like them, dress like them and had the same mop top haircut. I thought of him as the funny one and The Beatles as the cool ones, although they were great entertainers too. I saw all of their films and thought they were brilliant. George was underrated, he had this wonderful, dry sense of humour, whereas Ringo had this charm and pathos about him. I especially like his scenes with Eleanor Bron in *Help!* John was very good too – the banter between him and Wilfred Brambell in *A Hard Day's Night* is lovely, and he was good in *How I Won The War* as well. He could definitely have gone further as an actor.

I attended the same schools as Paul and Mike McCartney, Stockton Wood Infants, followed by Joseph Williams. I then went on to attend the same grammar school as John Lennon, which was Quarry Bank. We even shared the same headmaster, William Pobjoy. He was a very influential man, very liberal and ahead of his time. He would talk to us about John. In fact, it was Mr. Pobjoy that had helped him get into art school. He also encouraged the next generation of creative pupils – myself, Jude Kelly and Clive Barker included.

Growing up in Liverpool in the sixties and seventies was an exciting time. Jimmy Tarbuck's success had inspired me to believe that a working-class boy from my hometown could make it; and The Beatles' achievements had shown everyone else the same thing.'

LES DENNIS (Actor and comedian) - 2009

❛My sister is five years older than me, so it was her that really introduced me to The Beatles. My first memory related to them is singing *Till There Was You* when I was three years old, but all of their songs stir up memories for me. We would listen to the singles over and over again, not just the A-sides, but the B-sides too. They were the only B-sides in the house that we felt were worthy of being listened to. I mean, if you play a Frankie Vaughan B-side it's not really the same, is it! When I got my first job I went out and started collecting everything they ever did. I was in a band and somebody suggested that I should get *With The Beatles* to start with, as the songs were fairly simple to learn. I'd also read somewhere that a journalist had praised John Lennon's use of Aeolian cadences on *Not A Second Time*. That intrigued me too. Just like John, I still have no idea what Aeolian cadences are, but what does impress me is the rhythm guitar part he plays on *All My Loving*. How did he think of it? Did George Martin suggest it? He hadn't really been playing the guitar for that long, but he plays this amazingly difficult rhythm that I still can't do! Another interesting link I have is that I once played with a sixties band called The Rockin' Berries. As the name suggests, they were huge Chuck Berry fans, and they went to play in Hamburg at the same time as The Beatles. George Harrison used to watch them play from the side of the stage. Chuck Botfield, the lead guitarist, ended up teaching him how to play the intro lick to *Roll Over Beethoven* which, of course, appears on the album. It's amazing how all these things come full circle, isn't it. I suppose *With The Beatles* could really be regarded as *"Please Please Me 2"*, but I love its power and innocence. I also like the fact that a lot of the songs on it are ones they would have done at the Cavern. Apparently, Elvis told them that they resembled Children of The Damned on the cover!❜

‘February 9th 1964 – I will never forget that day. The population of America was around 180 million at that time. Of that 180 million, around 78 million people tuned in to watch *The Ed Sullivan Show*. That would never happen again. The Beatles took us by storm. I was thirteen years old and I remember that it was broadcast on Channel Two at 8pm. It knocked me off my feet. It's so hard to explain the impact The Beatles had on my generation, but for around two years after that they completely dominated us. After watching that show I knew what I wanted to do for the rest of my life. It was as a direct result of seeing The Beatles that I bought my first electric guitar. They are the sole reason I do what I do today.

In the States, this album was called *Meet The Beatles*, and there was no *Please Mr. Postman* or *Roll Over Beethoven* on it. The reason I love it is because of its energy, its idealism, its innocence and its fun. It's impossible to listen to without smiling from beginning to end. I enjoyed their later work, *Sergeant Pepper* and so on, but by then they'd had time to take in the whole Beatles phenomenon. Their records became more like art, more intellectual, whereas the early stuff was the sound of kids playing rock 'n' roll. Pure, unadulterated joy. People know me as a blues guy, but I'm a Beatle fuckin' maniac! To this day they are still the dominant influence on my musical taste. Whenever I'm in or near Liverpool I always take the tour and go down Mathew Street. My wife and I saw the Cirque Du Soleil show in Las Vegas which, of course, features Beatles music, and absolutely loved it.

The thing I always admired most about them was their unity, that bulletproof entity. It's what I always dreamed of experiencing as a musician. Sadly, it never really happened, but if I'd had the choice of being a Beatle or being Jimi Hendrix, I would have been a Beatle every time.’

WALTER TROUT (Solo artiste) - 2007/2011

‘It would have been around 1973 when I first started buying Beatles records for myself. I began with a couple of compilations and then moved on to the original albums. I was struck by the immediacy of this record, how well their rhythm 'n' blues influences, such as *Please Mr. Postman*, sat alongside their own material. To me, this recording captures the feel of a live act that have just come off the road and taken that same energy into the studio, which is pretty much where they were at the time. I'm almost certain that many of the cover versions would have dated back to the Hamburg days, and you can hear that tightness and familiarity come across in the recordings. *Money* would have to be my pick of them all. I think it's the best cover they ever did. With regard to their original material, a prime example would have to be *All My Loving*. Not only do you have Paul's craftsmanship as a songwriter, but there's George's great guitar solo and the amazing triplet effect that John plays on the rhythm guitar – just great!

I moved back to Edinburgh just before John was killed. I'd been out for a run and heard the news on the radio when I got in. I was very low for a long time after that, as were many people. We couldn't believe the senselessness in the way in which he died, especially as he was still a relatively young man with so much more to give.’

CHARLIE REID (The Proclaimers) - 2007/2008

‘In the early sixties there was an undercurrent of music happening in Liverpool. My brother was in a band called The Delrenas; they're the only Merseybeat band still going with all its original members. I'd go and watch The Beatles in The Cavern and at The Casbah in West Derby. Everyone would know everyone else – Cilla Black would take your coat in The Cavern, people would go into Brian Epstein's NEMS shop for their records. I knew Brian very well, he was a lovely man and we both had mothers called Queenie. Away from the nightlife, I worked at Ashley Dupre hair salon with Ringo's girlfriend, Maureen – the same Maureen he later married. She was a wonderful hairdresser and Ringo used to phone her from places like Amsterdam and Germany all the time. We were all in awe of that because it cost a pound a minute. Considering I was earning eight pounds a week, that was absolutely extortionate! Another thing I clearly remember is being at Silver Blades ice rink when *Love Me Do* came on. I remember thinking "that's it!" I knew they'd make it after that.’

HERBERT HOWE (Celebrity hairdresser) – 2008

‘The Beatles are such a fundamental part of my life. I love their melodies, their harmonies. *Beatles For Sale* is a boss album.’

PETER DOHERTY (The Libertines, Babyshambles and solo artiste) - 2008

'I regard *Beatles For Sale* as the final adolescent album that they made. It marked the end of their "fun" period. From now on their work would become less playful, particularly from *Rubber Soul* onwards. The number of cover versions on this LP may be attributed to the fact that they had already been working non-stop, especially on *A Hard Day's Night*, which had contained nothing but original songs. Included in their selection of covers here, you can hear their long-time appreciation of Carl Perkins on *Honey Don't* and *Everybody's Trying To Be My Baby*, as well John's amazing, screaming vocals on *Rock 'n' Roll Music* and *Mr Moonlight*. People from Liverpool have always been good screamers! I'm also pleased they chose *Words Of Love* by Buddy Holly, as they used to play a lot of his songs in The Cavern. Ending side one, we have *Kansas City / Hey Hey Hey*, which is probably my pick of the lot. I heard Little Richard do those two songs in exactly the same way, and although Paul isn't quite as flamboyant, he still does a great job of it. For all the fun and light-heartedness, *Beatles For Sale* also offers a darker side. You can hear the beginnings of Lennon's insecurities in *I'm A Loser* and *I Don't Want To Spoil The Party*. The former shows his new found love of Bob Dylan. To me, it sounds like a mixture of both Lennon and Dylan, therefore making it the perfect Byrds song! Then there's *Eight Days A Week*. It's not one of their best songs, but that phrase itself has become a part of the English language.'

SPENCER LEIGH (Merseybeat historian, author and radio presenter) – 2007

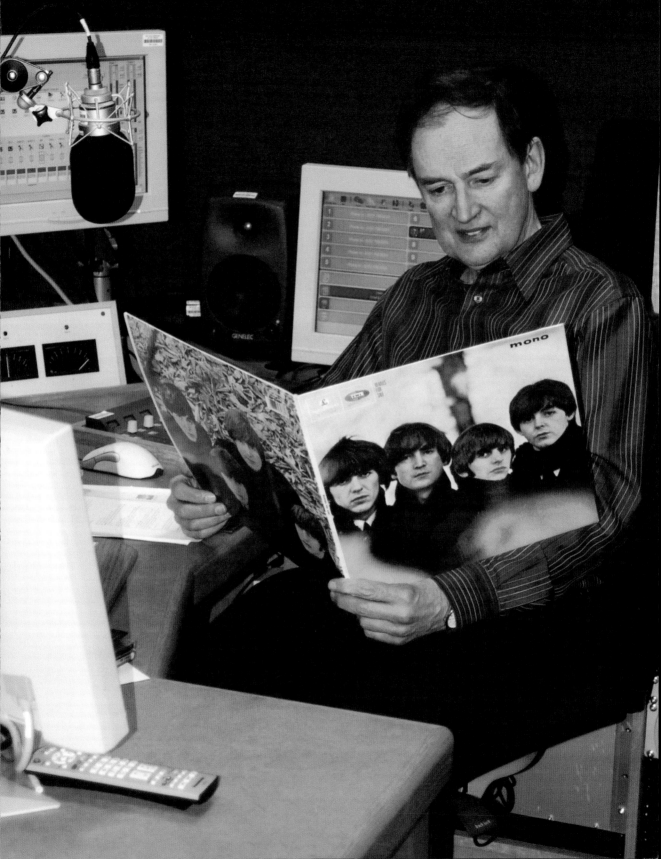

‘In the late fifties and early sixties I think I was the only Scouse lad who never played a guitar or owned a tea chest bass. Skiffle was all the rage at the time, so instead of playing it I would go and watch it. I'd go to The Cavern, which started as a jazz club, and the Iron Door, amongst others. Merseybeat took over from skiffle and I followed The Beatles right from the early days. I was the same age as them. The Remo Four were another favourite group of mine, as were Gerry and The Pacemakers. I bet poor old Gerry never realised he'd end up with a real pacemaker! I always felt sorry for the drummers. All the groups would do three or four gigs a night and the poor old drummer would have to lug his gear from one place to the next. If I'd ever joined a band I would have been the penny whistle player! Then there's the fashion. We'd all wear the collarless jackets and winklepicker boots, just like The Beatles. Those boots were great in a fight, what with the pointy toes on them. Anyway, when it came to the release of *A Hard Day's Night* I queued up to see it, just like everyone else. I thought it was sensational to see the progression the lads had made. They were no longer just singers, they were film stars too. They were obviously prolific songwriters, but I don't think any of them would have made it alone. The secret of their success was that mix, that chemistry. It's like making whisky. You have to have exactly the right blend for it to taste just right, and that's what happened with The Beatles.’

STAN BOARDMAN (Comedian) - 2007

❛I used to live on Anglesey in a place called Benllech, and all these Scouse girls would come down on holiday. Us young lads were always after them, you know. It was always Billy Fury this, Billy Fury that, Billy's lovely hair and all that, but then one year it was all gone. It was Beatles, nothing but Beatles. I went to see them in The Cavern and I thought they were great. We'd never seen anything like them, it was always "Someone and the Somethings" – Earl Preston and The T.Ts, Freddie Starr and The Midnighters, a front man and a backing group, but The Beatles were the first without a front man, the first to write their own songs. Pete was the drummer when I saw them. He was posing all the time, he wasn't really trying to be a drummer, he was trying to be a film star or something. The wonderful, beautiful Pete Best. Ringo was three-quarters more of a drummer, he was great with Rory Storm and The Hurricanes, and when he joined The Beatles he brought a lot more attack into the band. I loved the way he sang the Shirelle's song, *Boys*, on *Please Please Me*. He was as hungry as they were, whereas Pete didn't really mix with the rest of the band. I can be an introvert, but there's also another side to me. I don't think there was another side to Pete Best. And he was always with his mother. Even when he got fired out of The Beatles, he'd appear on TV shows with his mother. There are limits, surely! Anyway, they played all the standard Liverpool (cover) songs. Everybody did *Some Other Guy*, everybody did *Nothing Shaking But The Leaves on The Trees*, but the one-upmanship came if you knew who the original was by. If someone came on and said "we'd like to do *Fortune Teller* by Benny Spellman", everyone would go "oh, such knowledge", you know! The Beatles were not the first in Merseyside to do those songs, but they started the rush of excitement. Oriole Records came and signed everyone in the city. I think it was two or three days at the Grafton Ballroom where they recorded *This Is Mersey Beat*, a very good album.

It's probably because I got into The Beatles from the very beginning that I like their earlier albums best – *With The Beatles*, *A Hard Day's Night*, *Help!* – and that's probably why the most popular ones are the later ones. The younger people were joining in then, and there were more of them. *Rubber Soul* is where they started doing a lot of dope, and you can really tell (yawn). *Norwegian Wool?!* And *Sergeant Pepper* is very overrated. There are only two good songs on *Sergeant Pepper*, and they're two versions of the same song. I think that *A Hard Day's Night* and the other soundtrack albums get overlooked a lot, probably because they're thought of as 'soundtrack albums'. *I Should Have Known Better* reminds me of when George met Pattie Boyd, *If I Fell* and *And I Love Her* speak for themselves, *Things We Said Today* is one of the best things they ever did – the song itself, the chords, the majors and minors, and *You Can't Do That* is Lennon at his best. Probably the best song he ever recorded, certainly up there in the top three. I could do without *I'll Cry Instead* and *Anytime At All*, although *Any Time At All* is good in the chorus.

Some of the compilations that EMI have put out are lousy, the fucking *Yellow Submarine Songtrack* and the remastered digital rubbish. They weren't supposed to be heard that way, they were supposed to be heard mono. That's how they were recorded, that was what the world sounded like then. If the thing is recorded at a certain time period in the world then that's how you should hear it. When they re-released the mono set, I was a very happy man. Bought it immediately.

I was playing the guitar before The Beatles came along, but they inspired me to do my own stuff. They proved that you could play what you wanted – you didn't have to be fucking overdogs, underdogs could do it too. We proved the same thing ourselves. ❜

LEMMY (Motörhead) – 2011

❛I've always been a golden oldies type person, listening to the charts isn't really my cup of tea. I'd much rather hear stuff by people like Rod Stewart and, of course, The Beatles. I'm not an expert on which songs are on which albums, but I've always been aware of them. Their songs are classics. I'm a big Oasis fan too, and obviously their sound is not a million miles away. Noel and Liam are good friends of mine – they'd always play nothing but Beatles before going on stage. I'll sometimes play their stuff while I'm training, and I often listen to the CDs in the car. *Can't Buy Me Love* and *Tell Me Why* are two I like a lot. Another favourite is *All My Loving*, that's a real belter. My son is having guitar lessons and he loves computer games, so no doubt he will have a go on the Rock Band game before long. It just goes to show that they're as popular as ever.❜

RICKY HATTON (Former world champion boxer) – 2009

Oisin: "I think *A Hard Day's Night* is far more of an album than the likes of *Rubber Soul*. It glows with this raw, cheeky energy, yet the songwriting is fantastic too. I love the stripped back arrangements of *If I Fell* and *And I Love Her*, which has this lovely kind of Spanish guitar solo. I also find it quite a rootsy album, the harmonica in *I Should Have Known Better* is great."

Mark: "My favourite is *I'll Be Back*. Both these albums sound far less dated than *Sergeant Pepper*."

Oisin: "With *Help!* they began a new type of songwriting. *You've Got To Hide Your Love Away* shows the new direction they were taking with their lyrics, a more kind of Bob Dylan approach."

Mark: "Yes, I think *I've Just Seen A Face* is Paul's attempt at doing Dylan."

‘My world is all about show business and the theatre. Theatres, pantomimes, acrobats and ventriloquists, not rock 'n' roll, but I enjoyed some of The Beatles' music. I like songs to have a very strong melody, and *Yesterday* is my favourite of theirs. I met them a couple of times, worked with them a couple of times. I found them to be very affable, likeable people. George Harrison in particular was a very charming man, and I think that he was the best musician in the group. The first time I came across them, we were on the same bill at a charity night in Aintree. I didn't think much of them that night, but I do remember that one of them was playing a tea chest bass. A couple of years later, they'd made it all the way to the *Royal Variety Show*. I think that part of their success was down to luck, but they also managed to put a protective curtain between themselves and fame. They stayed down to earth, still four Liverpool lads having a lark.’

KEN DODD (Comedian) – 2011

❛It was through John and George that my association with The Beatles' films began. They both came to see me in *Oh What A Lovely War*, and afterwards George said: "You have to be in our film *(A Hard Day's Night)*, in fact you have to be in all our films cos my mum fancies you." So I was. We flew from London to the Bahamas for the filming of *Help!*, and the plane stopped in New York for fuel. Some official entered the cabin and asked: "Is there a Victor Spinetti on board?" John joked that they were going to deport me. Anyway, the official asked me to go to the door and give a wave to my fan club. The club had started while I was appearing on Broadway. Some of the people in the audience had recognised me from *A Hard Day's Night* and interrupted the play with screams of "he touched The Beatles!". I had to ask them from the stage to settle down and that I would see them after the performance. The after-show fan session became a regular thing and is the reason that Brian Epstein and the boys came to become card-carrying members of the Victor Spinetti Fan Club!

They were all so down to earth and I loved them for it. They were always happy to let me watch them at work too. I remember hearing *You've Got To Hide Your Love Away* as we ate bacon butties. John had no ego, he had no plan. He let things come to him. George, too, gave me a great present. I told him I was having trouble getting into Eastern music and he said: "Don't try Vic. Western music is all about maths, but you have to let Eastern music happen to you." I've never forgotten that. If you love The Beatles it is important that you try to live up to their lyrics. Look at their songs, there are none that are full of hate – no "murder this, kill that, jew this, fag that". People burnt Beatles records because John said they were "bigger than Jesus", but their music never talked about hateful things. It is those records that should be burnt. I once asked John what he considered to be his best lyric. He said: "That's easy, Vic. It's 'all you need is love'."

The Beatles produced an avalanche of poetry and melody which flooded over us. It's still there.❜

VICTOR SPINETTI (Actor) - 2008

‘If I close my eyes and listen to *Sergeant Pepper* I hear a studio recording, but if I close my eyes and listen to *Help!*, it sounds like a gig. I love the harmonies, the songwriting and the fact that it's not overproduced. In the early seventies these songs were still being played on the radio, which, as a five- or six-year-old, was how I first came to be aware of them.

With most of their other albums I like a handful of songs from each, but with *Help!* there's not a track I dislike. My favourite is probably *The Night Before*, and I also like Ringo's drumming on *Ticket To Ride*. He wasn't technically good as a drummer, but his simple yet effective approach was just what was needed. They wouldn't have sounded right if they'd had Keith Moon on drums.’

DARRIN MOONEY (Primal Scream) - 2008

❛In 1965 I was in the Special Forces and a friend and I decided to protest against Twentieth Century Fox messing up a beautiful village called Castle Combe. They had put up a dam to make it look like a lake for the filming of *Doctor Dolittle*, so we planned to use explosives to destroy it. We were only given a fine and a warning! That would have been unthinkable in the years that followed, the years when the IRA started bombing. The Beatles had brought out *Help!* while all this was going on, which is why I remember the album so sharply. Not only did the title track fit our situation, but I enjoyed other songs from it such as *Ticket To Ride* and *Yesterday* as well.❜

SIR RANULPH FIENNES (Adventurer) - 2008

❛*Help!* contains what I consider to be the definitive collection of Beatles songs. *Yesterday* has become a standard, much like Gershwin's songs, and *You've Got To Hide Your Love Away* and *Ticket To Ride* are great too. Besides that, I think the intro of *Help!* is the strongest opening you could possibly get to a song. I also love the little descending bit George plays on the guitar towards the end of each chorus. It's the song I always think of when I think of The Beatles. When people consider their songs, they tend to think Lennon/McCartney, but George was great too. He didn't have the pressure to come up with songs like John and Paul did, so he tended to write for all the right reasons, just as he continued to do in his solo career. As a guitarist he used so many different makes and models – Rickenbackers, Gretschs, Fender Telecasters, but whatever he used it always sounded like him. That's the secret of a great guitarist.

The epitome of The Beatles is definitely the music. They may have started out as good looking young guys that girls wanted to hang out with, but all of that fades away. When the girls stopped screaming The Beatles didn't disappear like some bands would. They continued to come up with the goods and that's why they're popular, even now. The Beatles and Bob Dylan are our Mozart and Beethoven, their songs are our classical pieces. Time judges whether or not people are deemed to be a success and The Beatles have more than achieved that. Bands in my hometown of Los Angeles still try to copy them today. They walk around with mop tops and whatever, but sadly they seem to have missed the important point – good songs, good music!❜

‘My first impression of The Beatles was that they looked amazing. John and George were very photogenic, it was easy to make them look good in front of the camera, but with Paul it was more difficult. He had such a baby face! He was always very polite though; in fact they all were. At that time my English was very bad. I could manage to say things like "do not smile", but I found it easier to actually get hold of them and place them how I wanted them to be – even their heads! They didn't mind, and their friendliness towards me never changed. When they were filming *A Hard Day's Night* I was invited to take photos and I actually stayed at George and Ringo's flat. Their looks, their music and the way they dressed are the things that made people want to go to their concerts; it's the same with bands today, but what the public really didn't get to see was the full extent of their warmth and intelligence.

Musically, I love George's solo work best, but to represent the four of them I would choose *Rubber Soul*. My favourite songs are *Norwegian Wood, In My Life* and *Nowhere Man*, but their personalities were always the most important thing. I didn't care if they were wearing collarless suits or whatever, I understood that Brian Epstein wanted them to look a certain way for money and fame, but all of that never changed the people they were on the inside.’

ASTRID KIRCHHERR (Photographer) – 2009

❛*Rubber Soul* is the album that turned The Beatles from chirpy Scousers into a revolutionary band. Prior to this album, despite the adulation and praise they'd received, you could still have put them on a package tour with The Dave Clark Five and people like that. This album revealed their darker side and transcended the mop top image. I love *Drive My Car*, especially the guitar solo, which was totally unique for the time. Another highlight is the mad medieval bit during *In My Life*. They were the best, no doubt. I think McCartney's songs are always better out of context than Lennon's; they stand up better as works in their own right and translate better when people cover them. I was in a taxi the other day, it was late at night, and there was some radio station on like Magic or Heart FM. Everything they played was nonsense, then *Yesterday* came on. It was head and shoulders above everything else. To me, McCartney was the one who was more of a composer in the traditional sense. The feeling he captured within that song is amazing, that kind of introspective melancholy. I'm still searching for my own *"Yesterday"*, but I'd like to think that *Love Is Here* comes close to expressing some of the same feelings.❜

JAMES WALSH (Starsailor) - 2008

❛When we went to France on tour, this LP had just come out. Steve (Marriott) and I briefly fell in love with two girls over there, so the song *Michelle* fits with those memories. In 1966, we all shared a house together and we would play this endlessly. It's funny because our kitchen/dining area was panelled in Norwegian wood, so that kind of fits with it too. Oh, and I really wanted John's jacket off the front cover! You know, for years I always thought that the back cover of *Rubber Soul* is actually the one that's on *Revolver*. I love that shot, the *Revolver* one, cos it looks like George has just told them all a joke and they're all going "you git!"❜

IAN McLAGAN (The Small Faces & The Faces) - 2002

‘To my mind, *Rubber Soul* has this kind of melancholy feeling running throughout it. If you look at the pictures on the front and back of the LP, they all, perhaps with the exception of Paul, look tired and a little fed up. By this time they had been worldwide stars for a couple of years, and I think it was beginning to take its toll. The drugs were also starting to kick in, not exactly taking over, but they were becoming a more prominent feature in their lives. With all that in mind, I think this showed them to be breaking away for the first time. George came into his own as a songwriter – with *If I Needed Someone*, he perfectly captured that definitive mid-sixties sound. It has a great overall feel and is vastly underrated. *In My Life* would also make my all time top five Beatles list. Aside from the obvious merits of the band, one thing I've noticed is their unique appreciation and feel for country music. Many of their contemporaries shared their love of rhythm 'n' blues, but with the country thing I think they pretty much stood out. Listen to *Act Naturally* from the *Help!* album, especially fantastic guitar solo. It wasn't just Ringo and George either, all four of them had that country thing happening at some point.’

CRAIG REID (The Proclaimers) - 2007/2008

‘I like *Rubber Soul* because I think it's their most uncluttered record. I also think it sounds very continental. The instrumental section in *Girl* sounds very Greek, and the other songs remind me of places I experienced when I was much younger – Germany, France and the Austrian mountains especially. It's the soundtrack to my memories of those places. I like some of the different instruments they used, such as the maracas. I'm always a fan of maracas in songs! I love the fuzz bass on *Think For Yourself*, the sitar in *Norwegian Wood* and Mal Evans' harmonium playing on *The Word*, which is possibly my favourite song on the album. When I was a kid I used to mess about with the balance of the record player. I'd listen to the guitars in one speaker and then all the harmonies in the other. 'Stereophonic geography' is what I called it. I also imagined that the photos on the back of the sleeve were songs. Paul's picture on the right hand side was *Drive My Car*, and George in the field was *Run For Your Life*, for some reason.

Revolver is another favourite album of mine. It has some amazing sounds on it. I think that their most interesting song guitar-wise is *And Your Bird Can Sing*. That riff is amazingly difficult . . . well it's probably not, but when you first sit down and try and work it out it is!’

GRAHAM COXON (Blur and solo artiste) – 2006

‘I think *Rubber Soul* was their first "band production", the first album they made for themselves rather than for the record company or to please the fans. They went back to a time when they were independent and that attitude continued with *Revolver*. In my mind, both of those records share a special connection. That connection was lost again on later albums.

In 1980, I was looking around for new songs and someone told me that John Lennon was working in the studio. Sadly, I said: "No, don't bother him"; and after that it was too late. Peter Yarrow from Peter, Paul and Mary told me the news of his death. We were only two blocks away from where it happened. My guitarist and I immediately went to Central Park. It was such an unbelievable shock.’

RICHIE HAVENS (Solo artiste) - 2007

‘Comedy and music have always gone hand in hand for me. Bands with a sense of humour and fun often find success through this, as well as their music. In my book, it's always a plus point for bands to make some other connection with their audience, and humour is a great way to do it. Look at the Arctic Monkeys and We Are Scientists for example, it somehow adds to the enigma.

When I was fifteen, I worked as a Saturday boy in a vintage clothing shop in Nottingham called Wild Clothing. We'd have music on all the time and I first heard most of The Beatles' back catalogue there. *The White Album* has always been overrated for me, perhaps due to hype and over-indulgence – part media, part Beatle to blame for that one. I'm probably wrong, but it has never been my cup of tea. *Rubber Soul* is my favourite due to its consistency. Their albums have often been accused of having weaker B-sides, but I think *Rubber Soul* improves in quality of song throughout. At fourteen tracks it is quite long, but I think it manages to sustain. One of my favourite tracks is *Wait* because of the energy in the chorus; it's like a really uplifting, driving love song. Conversely, I like the whimsy and pensive air of *In My Life*. I could do without *Norwegian Wood* at a push, but *Run For Your Life* really engaged me and my teenage angst and melodramatic attitude towards love. It's such an aggressive song, and what a way to finish – a threat-laden ditty filled with vitriol, thinly veiled as a pop song! It's the track that most reminds me of Lennon's solo work.

I've always had an affinity with drumming, and I think Ringo always had a raw deal. You only have to listen to *Tomorrow Never Knows, I Am The Walrus, Strawberry Fields* and *In My Life* to know there was real drumming talent going on in that band. The Beatles wrote consistently brilliant songs over a long period. And it's all about timing. Their arrival marked a new beginning in social culture.’

MATHEW HORNE (Actor) – 2009

Susanna: "We all love *Rubber Soul* and *Revolver* equally. The image of Paul smoking the ciggie on the back was almost pornographic to me as a six year old."

Vicki: "Phono porno!"

Susanna: "Almost! I later realised that *Drive My Car* wasn't as innocent as it first appeared to be too. Hello! 'Drive my car?' It's obviously about girl on top! It's one of my favourite songs, as is *The Word*. I love the album cover too. The suede jackets and long hair kind of made them look like Californian folk-rockers, and being Cali girls ourselves, we loved that. We could identify with it. Now, *Revolver*, I have an interesting story about that. John wrote the song *She Said She Said* after talking to a woman at a party. That party was after their Hollywood Bowl show and it took place round the corner from my house. Every kid in the neighbourhood knew about it and was desperately trying to get in to see The Beatles, me included. I was only six years old! Musically, I think it's the album that captures them at their heyday. They are the reason I do what I do and it's totally true that I play Rickenbacker guitars because of them."

Vicki: "I too was very young when I heard these albums, but *Rubber Soul* was where my sexual education began. For me, it's all about *Girl*. That sigh that John does in it! And *Run For Your Life* must be the most politically incorrect song ever, but I love it."

Debbi: "My favourites would be *Norwegian Wood* and *In My Life*. I also remember that I would spend hours looking at the cover of *Revolver*, all those tiny little pictures put together by Klaus Voormann. My brother had a way of fixing the record player so that you could hear the cowbell in *Taxman* really loud. It was my first real musical education."

Vicki: "Don't forget *And Your Bird Can Sing* – best guitar riff ever!"

THE BANGLES (Musicians) – 2008

❛The first time I saw The Beatles in Hamburg I was overwhelmed by them. They were so fresh, so funny, so young and, of course, they played great music too. The best thing about them was that they were fantastic individuals, as well as a fantastic foursome. I remained friends with them from that day. In 1966, John phoned me up and asked me what I thought should be on their next LP cover. He suggested that I should come to the recording studio and listen to the songs that would be on the album. I took photos and made sketches on paper, but I didn't know what I was going to do straight away. I always have to go through a long period of thinking about lots of different directions. I forget now how I decided on the final idea, but once I focused on it I got there pretty quickly. They all loved it on first sight. The only thing I had to change was two photos and that was it.

Aside from *Revolver*, I think that as a concept, the *Sergeant Pepper* cover is killer. I also think the photograph by Robert Freeman on *Beatles For Sale* is wonderful.❜

KLAUS VOORMANN (Artist and musician) - 2006/2000

ROBERT WHITAKER
1939–2011

As the Beatles' official photographer from 1964 to 1966, Robert's work included the image used on the reverse of the *Revolver* sleeve. It came as no surprise when he chose to pose with *Revolver* for this project, however, he informed me that he had no idea that any of his images would be used for such a purpose at the time he was taking them. Unfortunately, I was never able to complete a formal interview with Robert, as he passed away in 2011 after a long illness.

ROBERT WHITAKER (Photographer) – 2003

‘I sometimes find it difficult to talk about other people's work, as those recordings are very precious to those people, but I think *Revolver* is the only album that is truly "The Beatles". I find their other albums predictable for their time, even *Sergeant Pepper*. *Revolver* is their most interesting record in every regard, starting with the artwork that took you into the album. It always makes me laugh how the Parlophone pound sign is so prominent on the front cover. Is Parlophone the most important thing? I think that their later albums had too much outside input, orchestrations and so on, plus the songs began to sound very individual. Obviously their songs are perennial, but I think the strength is in the songs themselves rather than the recordings. Time and technology has reduced the immediacy of the music, the beats and so on, whereas I don't think that is necessarily the case for records like *Jumpin' Jack Flash*.

I find it interesting that they placed such restraint on their songs being used in adverts, especially in an era where young people grow up with adverts surrounding them. It could have helped to bring their music to younger generations much quicker, but I suppose they still got to hear it through their parents and the Anthology albums. I also admire the way in which Paul McCartney still plays the songs live. With the status and success he has, it's easy just to sit with four Rolls Royces on the drive and not bother, but what he does shows a love and respect for the songs. I like that. ’

EDDY GRANT (Solo artiste) - 2008

❮*Revolver* was a real breakthrough record in music. It was the first psychedelic LP and featured numerous songs which could not be reproduced on stage. *Eleanor Rigby* and *Yellow Submarine* both tell a story – the first poignantly, the second is a classic adventure. I like them both. *Got To Get You Into My Life* is very like the songs they used to sing in The Cavern, but an original, and *Here, There And Everywhere* is just lovely. I like the earlier LPs better than the later ones. Apart from individual tracks, the later LPs start to lose me.

When I went for my interview at Oxford University, I didn't hide my Liverpool accent. The interview board at St Anne's College were clearly intrigued. There was clearly an element of "we've got to have her" about the gentle questioning and, in the end, they offered me a scholarship. Couldn't go wrong that day! If The Beatles could make it, then any Scouser could. Paul was very musical and so was George, but in a different vein. John was a visionary and Ringo added humanity to the mix. Overall, the sum was greater than the parts, as has been shown since the breakup.❯

EDWINA CURRIE (Former Member of Parliament) - 2010

‘This record saved my life, it really did. When it came out I was in St Tropez feeling really low and depressed. I remember that it was released the same time as The Four Tops' *I'll Be There (Reach Out)* and between the two of them I felt lifted again. My favourite song is *And Your Bird Can Sing*. No one's ever done a cover of that one.’

SIR ELTON JOHN (Solo artiste) - 2002

❛My musical heroes tend to be people like Chris Cain and Jimi Hendrix, but as composers I think The Beatles were incredible. I love *Revolver* because it's a mixture of straight pop songs, things like *Taxman*, alongside the more off-the-wall experimental songs they had begun to produce at that time. *Eleanor Rigby* is one of my favourites. I love the arrangement and the fact that it has a lot of soul – even Aretha Franklin covered it. We talked a lot about this album in my drama class at college. I couldn't believe how innovative they had been, things such as putting John's voice through a Leslie speaker on *Tomorrow Never Knows* and the mixing of Western and Eastern influences. The thought of being that inventive makes me speechless. There's nobody who can write like them these days. A lot of modern music consists of people writing a song and then paying an artiste to sing it, but they could write and play. In my band we do a few covers, but Stevie Wonder and The Beatles are among the artistes we would never touch. It's like walking on sacred ground and we just won't go there.❜

OLI BROWN (Solo artiste) – 2009

‘I have fond memories from when I was small of listening to The Beatles' singles. My favourite song was and still is *Thank You Girl*, but unfortunately that didn't make an album. I've always preferred the kitschy, poppy Beatles to the psychedelic stuff. I find a lot of that a bit too drug induced and weird. I was only seven or eight at the time and it didn't relate to me at all. I sort of forgot about The Beatles in the eighties, when they were pretty much regarded as ancient history, but I had a kind of reawakening when I became a songwriter myself. I was completely in awe of what Lennon and McCartney had achieved – so many fantastic songs in such a short period of time. I decided to learn more about them. Somebody suggested that I should listen to the *Revolver* album, which bridged the pop era that I loved and the psychedelic era that I didn't. I think the string arrangement on *Eleanor Rigby* is amazing – such a simple idea just to have a string quartet and vocals, yet it's so effective. How lucky they were to have George Martin to do things like that for them, and don't we all wish we'd thought of it first!’

ANDY McCLUSKEY (OMD) – 2002/2008

'I first met The Beatles when they came to see us at The Station Hotel in Richmond. I thought John and Paul had "it" from the very beginning. It was obvious they'd studied The Everly Brothers and stuff to perfect the harmonies they had. I also thought that Paul was a very good bass player. George and Ringo improved over time. In the beginning, George would be asking Keith how to play Chuck Berry riffs and stuff, but he definitely got better, as did Ringo. They were always very pop and we were more blues and soul, so there was definitely room at the top for both of us. Any rivalry between us was created by the media and fans, they were trying to make us like the Mods and Rockers, whereas in actual fact we were always friends. Brian Jones played on a couple of sessions for them and they did some stuff with us on *We Love You*, although back then bands didn't really collaborate like they do now.

Sergeant Pepper was brilliant because it was so different from anything else. The final track, *A Day In The Life* means a lot to me because it was about Tara Browne, someone who I used to hang out with in London. Most bands build an album around the singles and then put in some fillers, whereas The Beatles' singles didn't even appear on many of the albums. Equally, you could have used many of their album tracks as singles. It's crazy that they didn't. I still listen to their music, I have them on my iTunes. You forget about certain songs like *Norwegian Wood*, but then it comes on and surprises you; you remember what a good song it is.

It's amazing that now, forty years on, my girls, who are 13, 12 and 10, love Beatles music too. They like The Stones, but they're crazy about The Beatles, particularly the *Love* album. I can't really hear that much difference in some of the *Love* tracks, but I suppose it puts all your favourite bits together in one place. I think the secret of their longevity is that their songs are easy to remember, they have nice melodies and kids from any generation will always pick up on that.'

BILL WYMAN (The Rolling Stones) - 2008

Jayne: "The first record that me and my mum ever bought was *She Loves You*. I remember going to buy it when it came out. We couldn't afford a lot, but we went up and bought that. Gosh! We played it over and over again. Mum was a Beatles fan too. I like all of their music, but *Sergeant Pepper* stands out as the most interesting album that they made. I stayed with their poppy stuff for a while, but came back to their psychedelic stuff when I was a bit older and had begun to listen to different kinds of music."

Chris: "They came from a society where people listened to albums in a different way. I think everyone's about hit singles these days, whereas The Beatles, certainly with their later work, produced albums where there was a connection or thread. With *Sergeant Pepper* they went from basic playing to studio sampling and really started the new culture of changing the sound of music. For one of our tours, we did a whole production number based upon their songs, one of which was *Lucy In The Sky With Diamonds*."

Jayne: "We also did a piece for the World Professional Championships which used two John Lennon songs – *Revolution* and *Imagine*. I actually got a letter from Yoko after that performance. It had taken place in America and she'd seen it on TV. She said that she really enjoyed our interpretation of the music and thought that John would have approved of it, which was really nice."

Chris: "Beatles songs are always good to skate to. They're popularist, the words always tell a story and it's the music that we both grew up with. The music that you listen to between the ages of about 12 and 20 kind of stays with you for the rest of your life."

JAYNE TORVILL & CHRISTOPHER DEAN (Olympic figure skating gold medallists) - 2010

❛Like a lot of people, I first heard The Beatles through adults playing the records. Little kids can enjoy songs such as *Birthday* or whatever, but then their work has mass appeal throughout every stage of life. I think that's the thing that sets them apart from bands like The Rolling Stones and The Kinks, whose songs were more aimed at a particular age group. I like *Sergeant Pepper* because it's the first exciting sound of them experimenting. They had earned the right to do an album like this, and for the first time they didn't have to worry about performing it live. Every song is its own individual thing, which is something our band takes inspiration from. They risked cohesion to bend the form, and I hope that we can do that too.❜

BENJAMIN GRUBIN (Hockey) - 2009

❛*Sergeant Pepper* doesn't age like some of the other albums. When you think of the equipment they had, it's amazing that they were able to produce something so advanced. My favourite songs are probably *She's Leaving Home*, which can make me cry, and the title track, which features an amazing McCartney vocal. Several bands tried to re-create the entire album for its 40th anniversary, and most of it was terrible! They were just not able to record in that live situation, which was how it was done in 1967. It's a testament to George Martin's precise recordings that they had such good sound sources to build the *Love* album, of which *Being For The Benefit of Mr. Kite* is my favourite part. A lot of my work revolves around singing Beatles songs, but I can still get in the car after the gig and listen to one of their CDs. Why is that? I have also used some of their songwriting techniques in my own work. A prime example would be the verses in *Lucy In The Sky With Diamonds*, where the guitar line doubles the vocal melody. It just sounds so trippy and great. Overall, Pepper is just a great piece of timeless psychedelia.❜

CHRIS O'NEILL (George Harrison in the film *Backbeat*) - 2007

❛Before all the British blues stuff took off in the mid sixties, Hank Marvin and George Harrison were my biggest guitar heroes. I went to see The Beatles in Belfast when I was eleven years old – I went on my own and was deafened by the screams. Around that time, I would sit in my room and try and work out their songs. There was always such a melodic content to them, which taught me a lot, and George's solos were constructed like mini masterpieces. I loved his inventiveness, things such as using the volume knob to create the guitar sound you can hear in *I Need You*. He didn't just show off, he actually thought about what he was going to play, then composed something unique that became part of the song. The introduction to *Here Comes The Sun* is one example, and another is the *Hard Day's Night* solo. That one is actually very fast for its time. There were a lot of flashy players around in the sixties, but George wrote solos that you could sing, and that's exactly what The Beatles needed. I would never have dreamt that I would end up working with him. I actually met and worked with all of The Beatles, except John Lennon, but to me, George was a phenomenal musician. We became very good friends and he let me play all his Beatle guitars, which he kept on the wall in his house. I discovered that I'd been playing the opening chord to *A Hard Day's Night* wrong. George showed me the correct shape and, without thinking, I said: "Are you sure?" I always loved the 12-string Rickenbacker sound, that kind of jangly sound that The Byrds also used. I can't really picture myself playing a Gretsch though.

Sergeant Pepper is my favourite album because it was so different to anything they'd done before. Considering the recording equipment they had, they made the very best of it and took it further than anyone else. It was their version of psychedelia, so many different styles, and with the songs running into each other it was almost like a concept album. Not quite, but almost. As well as great songs, like *Getting Better* and *Within You Without You*, they were also having a bit of a laugh – *Lucy In The Sky With Diamonds* – L.S.D. – ha ha ha! There were all those amazing sounds too. Me and my friends would listen to it over and over again at the youth club. It completely "blew our minds". I was only in my early teens at the time, but I totally got it.❜

GARY MOORE (Thin Lizzy and solo artiste) - 2008

❛If it wasn't for these four guys, I wouldn't be here today. They forced me to out and buy a guitar. They are responsible for my career. Anyone who is fifty years old and says that they weren't influenced by The Beatles is lying. Their harmonies and attitude spoke to me, they still do. I also have to mention how much I love Paul McCartney's bass playing, because I sometimes think that it gets overlooked. He was the best bass player of his generation. When I heard *Sergeant Pepper* I was still in school. I loved the way the opening song morphed into *With A Little Help From My Friends*, especially with all the applause and everything. It matched the film I had in my head. Everybody has their own film of *Sergeant Pepper*, right? I love the whole journey right from the very beginning to *A Day In The Life*.❜

GLENN HUGHES (Deep Purple and solo artiste) – 2008

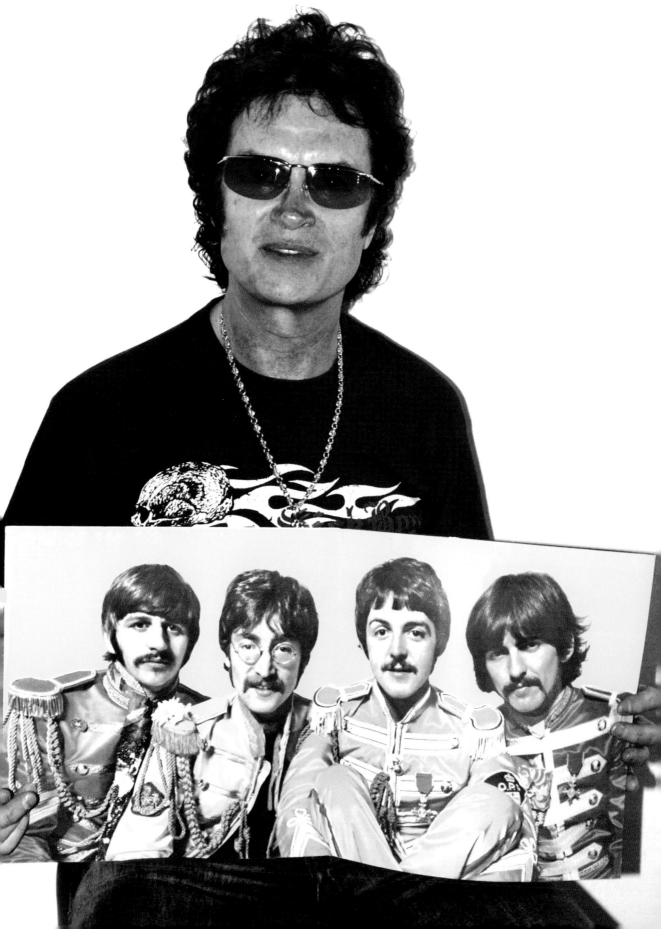

❛The Liverpool that The Beatles came from was a very sparse place, but they had a "let's just get on with it" attitude. They remind me of an auntie who doesn't have much money but always puts on a nice spread for everyone. People got through the Second World War by listening to cheerful big band music like Glenn Miller, and The Beatles created a similar sense of euphoria and being throughout the social changes of the sixties. Their music made the masses feel uplifted and "well fed", just like that auntie who's looking after her family and making sure everyone's OK. Fame was just a by-product of that. It was their reward. People were prepared to exchange cash for a piece of their imagination, but they never let it affect their sense of "getting on with it". To me, this album cover shows them as typical Scousers away from home. They've pushed beyond the glass ceiling of where they live and now they're having a laugh at authority. The next picture would probably show them pulling moonies. I find it a bit disappointing, a bit lacking in effort compared to the likes of the *Sergeant Pepper* cover, but the album itself is enjoyable. Their song collection is like a buffet, there's so many different things on offer, you have to try it all. What I mean is, you're not just going to go for the gateaux and ignore the peanuts, are you! When I listen to *All You Need Is Love* it makes me feel like John is addressing us all as his children, it goes back to that sense of an extended family. That's a very Liverpool thing.❜

STOK (Graffiti artist) - 2008

86

❛When I was fourteen I used to sell football programmes, and with my first wage packet I bought the American import of *Magical Mystery Tour*. I got it from HMV in Sutton High Street. In Britain, *Magical Mystery Tour* was originally only an EP, so all you got was the first six songs that are on the album. If you wanted to hear the rest, which included *Strawberry Fields, Hello Goodbye* and *Penny Lane*, you'd have to own the singles. Getting hold of them in 1971 was virtually impossible, and sadly for me I'd stopped buying Beatles singles when the guys grew moustaches. In my eleven-year-old wisdom I'd decided they'd gone a bit too wacky, so I changed allegiance and followed The Monkees instead. I was back on board when *Lady Madonna* came out, but *Magical Mystery Tour* gave me my only chance to hear the fantastic songs I'd missed out on in between. I love the whole sound of the record en masse – the orchestra in *Strawberry Fields*, the flutes in *Fool On The Hill* and John's brilliant vocals on *I Am The Walrus*. My favourite overall song is probably *Your Mother Should Know*. It's not an earth-shattering piece of music, just a really lovely little ditty. I'll nearly always toy around with it when I'm sitting at a piano.

I've been playing George Harrison for over 25 years now, and it's really made me appreciate the little touches he added to John and Paul's songs. If you listen to what he plays after the "and you know that can't be bad" line in *She Loves You*, that's a nice example of what I mean. The best example I can probably think of is the riff he puts at the end of the choruses in *Help!* It's just so fast and took me a while to work out. It was like the Holy Grail, and once I'd got it I couldn't stop playing it. Even now, I still think about it when I perform it.❜

ANDRÈ BARREAU (The Bootleg Beatles) - 2007/2008

‘*Strawberry Fields Forever* holds a special place in my heart. When I was seventeen, I left my native Denmark to come and live in London. I was just starting out in tattooing and life, and it was quite a baffling time. We used to go out to Surrey, to a beautiful landscape of fields and stuff. We had some wild times and, should you make a film about it, *Strawberry Fields* would be the soundtrack to that entire era. Another significant song for me is *Penny Lane* which, of course, is about thinking back to where you came from. Obviously, at that time in my life there was quite a lot of feeling homesick, so I could really relate to that. The whole album has a very nostalgic feel to it. It's also fitting that I'm speaking about those songs at a time when I've kind of reached the stage I wanted to be at back then.

The Beatles represent an era that people look back on with fond memories, even people who weren't there. They, more than anyone else, stand for a time in British history where a lot of changes were made. Not only will their music be forever associated with that time, but they were also the band who fronted a lot of those changes – hair growing and fashion, for example. I don't think any other band sums up that era as well as they do. They deserve to be the ones we should remember the most. ’

DAN GOLD (Celebrity tattoo artist) - 2009

Chas: "One of the first things I remember about The Beatles is when a band I was in called The Outlaws played a gig with them in Bootle. They were actually second on the bill to us! Anyway, what struck me about them was their harmonies. Not only did they blend together beautifully, but they could reach the real high notes. They used to do songs by the girl groups like *Please Mr Postman* and they could reach those top notes! They were also the first group I noticed who sang in their own accents. Most bands at that time would try to sound American. One funny memory I have is of being with the guys on their last European tour. Paul played *Yellow Submarine* to me and looked me straight in the eye for my reaction afterwards. I didn't know whether to laugh or what. Was it a joke? In the late sixties I was in The Bahamas with The Rebel Rousers. We only had about three LPs with us and *The White Album* was one of them. We spent three months over there, and in all that time I never got bored of that record. My favourite track would probably be *I'm So Tired*. The Beatles put the melody into rock 'n' roll and I don't think there've been any major changes since . . . except, maybe, punk."

Dave: "I remember hearing them on some radio show. I also remember that everyone at the time thought that 'Beatles' was a stupid name. I'd heard tales from a friend of mine who had been in Hamburg with them. He said they were a crazy bunch who would jump off the amps and stuff during their performances. I was in Hamburg myself when I bought the *White Album*. I was touring with Slim Whitman and had bought one of those fold-up record players – blow up speakers and all that, and we had the *White Album* on a lot. I remember that *Rocky Raccoon* was a favourite amongst us all. I also used to read the NME and I remember once reading an article about Paul McCartney with the headline 'Great Bass Player? Not Me!'. In the interview Paul played down his bass technique by saying that all he did was follow Ringo's bass drum pattern. I don't think that's true at all, most of his bass lines are very melodic and I don't think he's ever produced a duff one. A good example is the bass line to *Something*. He once told me he liked the bass part I played in *Rabbit*, and I told him that was a great compliment coming from him. I also notice that he hasn't changed his bass sound in all these years – still a thumping sound played with a plec. I think the secret of The Beatles' success is that they kept it coming all the time. They never ran out of good songs, and that kept them head and shoulders above the rest."

CHAS HODGES & DAVE PEACOCK (Chas & Dave) – 2006

❛Preceding the *White Album*, Bob Dylan released an album called *John Wesley Harding*, a stripped down record that possibly set the tone for what The Beatles would do next. With the *White Album* they too returned to a more simplistic approach, removing themselves completely from the grandeur of *Sergeant Pepper*. I like the mixture of genres on the record. My favourite tracks include *Everybody's Got Something To Hide Except Me And My Monkey*, *Why Don't We Do It In The Road* and the fantastic *Happiness Is A Warm Gun*, which I think is one of the cleverest songs ever – the title, the changes in time signature, the fact that it starts off on a journey and doesn't go back to the beginning – everything. I also think it's very dark lyrically, whereas my second favourite album would be *Rubber Soul* for completely different reasons. I find it full of humour and sarcasm. It also inspired The Charlatans to use more tambourine!

The Beatles definitely inspired the "baggy" movement in the early nineties. You can hear how songs like *Strawberry Fields* and *Tomorrow Never Knows* influenced the sound of bands like us and The Stone Roses. Then they went and did it all again with Britpop! The story of the Beatles is the perfect rock story, and it still continues to this day.❜

TIM BURGESS (The Charlatans) - 2006

❮I first heard the *White Album* while I was at university in London. It always reminds me of that time in my life, becoming a young man. I always loved the song *Blackbird*, and when I found out it was about a woman in the black civil rights movement, it made it all the more poignant. It's things like that which show you the genius of their writing – turning something so profound and serious into this beautiful song. It's very metaphysical too, the representation of this lovely little bird that's come through all the turmoil and is now flying.

When I meet people for the first time, they tend to think I'm from Scotland or Ireland. When I say "no, Liverpool", it'll take them a second or two and then they'll go "oh, yeah, The Beatles!" It can sometimes help to break the ice. Their career is a massive inspiration to anyone from the city, especially artistes. They followed their passion, they followed their dream. They were all very creative and they believed in pursuing that kind of path rather than working on the docks or being builders or plumbers, not to take anything away from those jobs, but they aspired to a more creative side of life. They're like a beacon to everyone, but the fact that they're from Liverpool makes it that bit more special.❯

STEPHEN GRAHAM (Actor) - 2010

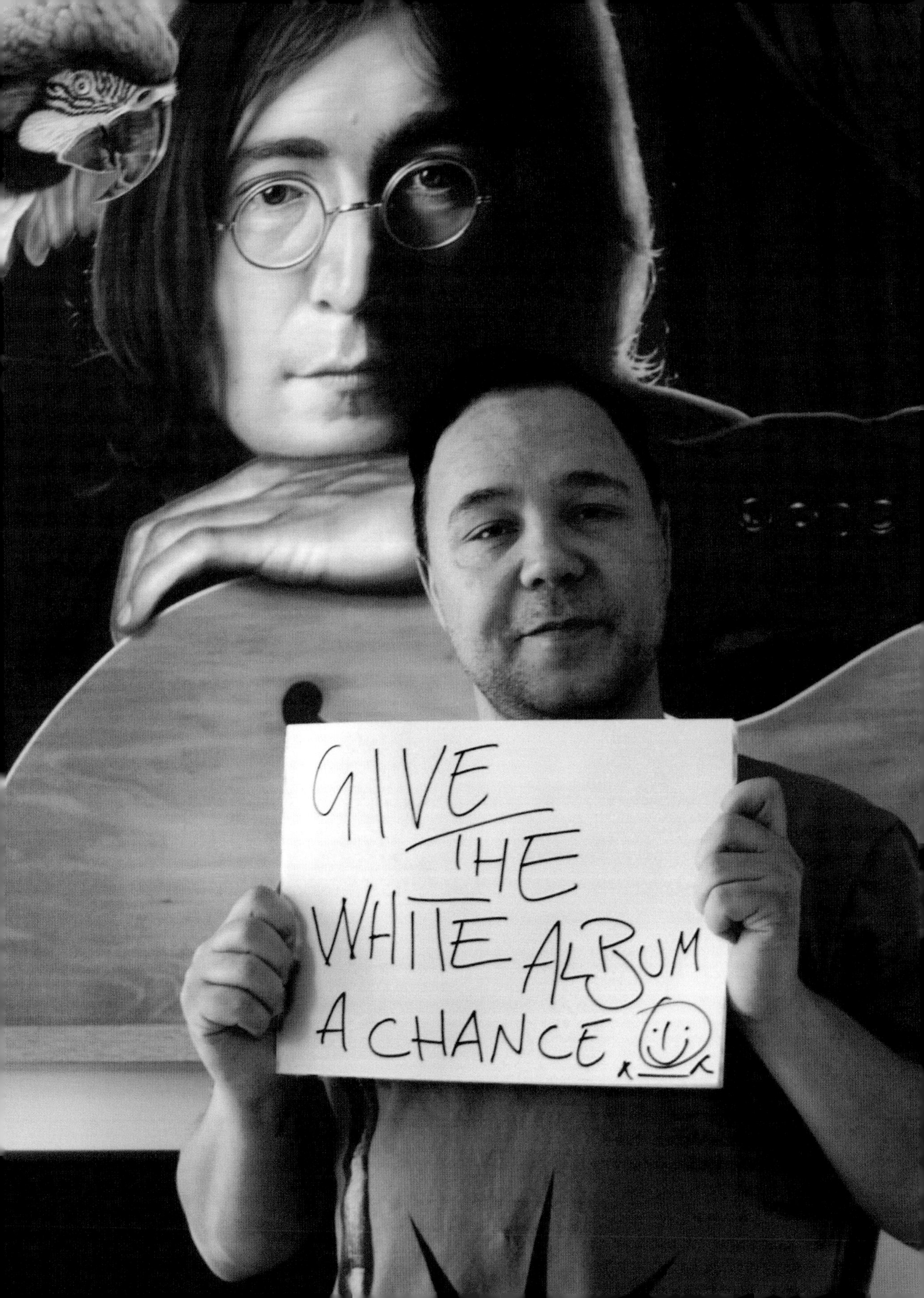
GIVE THE WHITE ALBUM A CHANCE

❛There are three things that make me proud to be British – the BBC, the NHS and The Beatles. When I was about four and my brother about six, we used to pretend to be them. He used to be George and I used to be Ringo. I think it was because we were from Birmingham that we had that kind of self-deprecation where we never felt that we were good enough to be John and Paul! I also clearly remember when The Beatles split. I was five by this time, and it was already a memorable time in my life. We had moved to Dorset for a year after the death of my grandfather, and I can still see the front page of whatever newspaper it was. Paul had a beard and a white Arran sweater on. He and Linda were each holding one of Heather's hands, swinging her between them. The headline was "Paul Quits".

The first time I heard the *White Album* I didn't like it. By this time I was about ten. My brother had got hold of it and he tried to persuade me that it was their best album because it was called *The Beatles*. I didn't agree. Growing up when I did, children were attracted to the early Beatles, watching them in films like *A Hard Day's Night* and *Help!* and, of course, the *White Album* sounded nothing like that. There's no *Yellow Submarine* is there? More sort of "songs about heroin"! As I got a bit older and began listening to them properly, the *Blue Album* helped me to get into their later stuff. Now I would say that, alongside Neil Young's *Decade*, the *White Album* is my favourite album of all time. It's like a show, every song is so different. In some ways they sound more like a rock band, I mean what other Beatle song sounds like *Helter Skelter*? Then there's *Revolution #9*, which used to be a good laugh when we were lysergically challenged, and George has some good songs on there too. *Long Long Long* is a beautiful song with a disturbing ending. All of the songs are very charming in their own different ways, but *Don't Pass Me By* isn't Ringo's best. In fact, it's pretty rubbish! My whole musical being is steeped in The Beatles. There's a song of ours called *Get Away* which definitely nicks from *Dear Prudence*, but I think a lot of people have nicked from that song!❜

SIMON FOWLER (Ocean Colour Scene) - 2010

‘By this point in their career The Beatles weren't too concerned with writing hit songs any more, they just wrote what they felt like writing. Having said that, you could take most of the songs from this album and they would still be big hits. An average song for The Beatles, say *Sexy Sadie*, would be a triumph for any other band. If I'd written it I'd certainly want it as a single! But The Beatles weren't too bothered and that's what I like about this record. My favourite tracks are the more earthy ones like *Mother Nature's Son* and *Yer Blues. Yer Blues* has a great guitar sound and the drums are really good too. I also really love the mad cowbell on *Everybody's Got Something To Hide Except Me And My Monkey.*’

DAVE McCABE (The Zutons) - 2006

'Some people consider the *White Album* a little hard to digest, there's a large amount of songs on it and I believe George Martin suggested that they should have made it a single album. I doubt that any record company would release it in its original form today. You can also sense that the band are drifting apart, but it's that tension that makes it an amazing album in my eyes. I think that Lennon in particular always wrote his best songs when he was tense or angry. I suppose there are a few tracks I would leave off, *Ob-La-di-ob-la-da* and *Piggies* for example, but there are also some tracks that don't get the credit they deserve. George's *Long Long Long* is a beautiful, subtle song that you will hardly ever hear mentioned, *Revolution #9* gives us a primitive version of sampling, showing that The Beatles were innovative with sounds and not just songs, then there's *Helter Skelter*, which is like a prototype Led Zeppelin. I also really like Ringo's drumming on *Don't Pass Me By*. Overall, I find 1968-1969 to be their most interesting period. The *Yellow Submarine* album deserves a mention for *It's All Too Much*, another great George song, and *Hey Bulldog*, which has an amazing vocal and dirty guitar sound. I really love the fact that John's guitar tone got dirtier and dirtier during this period; you can hear how it contrasts against George's and Paul's when they alternate guitar riffs in *The End*. In a way I'm glad that I was only able to hear these albums long after they were made. Reading about the history of the recordings and having that background knowledge makes me appreciate them more than if I'd been around to buy them on the day they were released.'

BARRIE CADOGAN (Touring musician) - 2008

❛I was at home one day in 1966, in the days when there were no cars on the Edgware Road on a Sunday, and I was sitting crossed legged on my Japanese rug. Suddenly the doorbell rang and I got up to answer it. At the door was Paul McCartney, wearing a suit with no tie, very much like the *Abbey Road* cover later on. I invited him in and he sat down. I'd heard he'd been writing recently, so I asked him what he'd got. He played me *Eleanor Rigby* followed by *Yellow Submarine*, which had a missing bit. "You're good at children's songs," he said, "can you think of something?" I told him I would need to think, so I went in another room for five minutes where I came up with the line "sky of blue, sea of green". Shortly afterwards, the doorbell rang again. I went to answer it with Paul following on behind me. At the door this time was a policeman. He didn't recognise me, but turned to Paul and said: "Is that your Aston Martin with the door open, one wheel on the kerb, three wheels on the road and music blaring out?" Paul said that it was, to which the policeman replied: "Well, if you give me the keys I will go and park it for you." Typical, I thought, those Beatles are always being treated like royalty!❜

‘When I was a kid my mum worked at a cinema and she'd often take me to watch films there. I would usually see a John Wayne film or something like that, and she'd always take time to explain a bit about what was going on and the moral of the story. When I went to see *Yellow Submarine* she didn't do that, she just left me to figure it out for myself. I didn't have a clue what was going on, but I loved the look of it, the weirdness of it. After that I got hold of the soundtrack via a family member. I would listen to it in the hope it would help me make sense of the cartoon. I decided that the day I understood *Yellow Submarine* was the day I'd become a man. I still don't understand it!

A great deal of the soundtrack is instrumental, composed by George Martin. Growing up around music, I always understood and appreciated the role that a producer played in a recording, much like Phil Spector's contribution to Motown. I am curious to hear the *Love* album that George and his son worked on, but having heard remixes of Bob Marley's catalogue I'd be a bit apprehensive about whether I'd like it or not. I always preferred The Beatles' later period than the early "hysterical" period. Even *they* admitted that all that screaming had a detrimental effect on the music. I can also identify with the later period more. I can see parallels with Rastafarian culture – messages of peace, love and growing your hair.’

BENJAMIN ZEPHANIAH (Poet) - 2007

'People seem to think that *Let It Be* was symptomatic of The Beatles' break-up; however, I think they were in the process of rediscovery, but other things got in the way. It could be compared to series 13 of *Top Gear* – very ad lib in parts, perhaps over-produced in others. People's opinions are similarly divided. I like the sort of live feel to it, some of it sounds like jamming. My favourite song is probably *I've Got A Feeling*, but some of the album sounds very produced, such as *The Long And Winding Road*. I've been told that McCartney wanted that as just the piano. I learned that song by ear as a boy, and from that I began to understand seventh chords and the like. I've also drummed to it, and to *Hey Jude*, not to mention singing lots of their songs, under the influence of beer, to karaoke machines.

As composers I think they were great, you can't fool listeners in the long run. It's been said that the true test of great music is its indestructibility in the hands of arrangers, and Beatles tunes prove this to be the case. Lennon was the better poet in my view, but McCartney the better tunesmith. Melody is the key to their longevity, although I would say that *Sergeant Pepper* is an overrated album. It's now just accepted hype, but I actually preferred The Beach Boys' *Pet Sounds*.'

JAMES MAY (TV presenter) - 2009

‘When I was an art student, I used to have these five-hour sessions in the studio at college. During that time I would constantly listen to The Beatles' Anthology CDs. They would be on in the background all day, over and over. As a musician I found it interesting to listen to the way they constructed the songs, the way the songs developed and the way they communicated with each other in the studio. I was always trying to guess which version of a song would end up on the album – sometimes I was very surprised at the final version. From there, I wanted to see them play live. I got the Anthology DVD series, and although there's lots of footage of them playing on TV shows, they look nervous and tense most of the time. When it comes to the concert footage, you can hardly hear a note over the screaming. My mom was actually part of all that, she went to Shea Stadium, but I didn't want that, I wanted to really see and hear them as musicians. *Let It Be* is like sitting in on a Beatles jam session. I also think it's their most cohesive album since *Beatles For Sale*. After *Beatles For Sale* they became more conscious about making each track something special or different. If you look at a song like *Strawberry Fields*, which they recorded about six times adding all kinds of horns, bleeps and strings, the songs on *Let It Be* are the complete opposite. Some of them aren't even finished.

In 1969, music was changing a lot. Psychedelia had gone in the toilet, Eric Clapton had broken up Cream, and The Band had inspired a lot of people to go back to the roots of rock 'n' roll, including The Beatles. They were no longer interested in building upon their greatness. You can hear The Band's influence a lot. It's in the country gallop of *Get Back*, the guitar turn-arounds in *I've Got A Feeling* and in George's *For You Blue*, which features a great slide solo by John. I really liked the way John would mess about with timings and stuff in his guitar playing; he was a smart guitarist, he knew what he was doing. I also think that Paul McCartney basically invented melodic bass playing in rock 'n' roll. I used to have a sticker of him on my bass. We both started out as guitarists who were persuaded to swap to bass by our band members, and I felt a lot in common with him over that. He had the professionalism not to get bitter about it, he got on with it and did the job as well as he possibly could. I took a lot of inspiration from that and I try to do the same thing. I can also understand why he wanted to go back and change some of the *Let It Be* album. The strings and voices on *The Long And Winding Road* can be too much, particularly when they had envisioned a less rich-sounding record. For me, it's the no-frills approach that makes it a great album. Everybody knows about their innovation, the way they changed culture, their songwriting, but I don't think they were always fully appreciated as musicians. During *Let It Be* they may have been tense personally, but they were at their most relaxed musically.’

NICK ACKERMAN (The Virgins) - 2009

‘The Beatles were really falling apart by this stage and put very little effort into the recording, yet the songs are still wonderful, even if they're mostly works in progress rather than properly finished. In those days I only knew The Beatles through their singles on the radio, I heard their albums much later. I already knew *Get Back*, which is great, basic rock 'n' roll, and *Let It Be* itself, which I found sad but uplifting. *Don't Let Me Down*, the B-side of *Get Back* should have been on the album and *Maggie May* is just a scrap but it gets a taste of Liverpool in there. Some of the other tracks are pretty rough too, especially as they were released after *Abbey Road*, which is so polished, but that's OK. In a way, the album does just what the film was intended to do, it gives you a glimpse of a real-life working band. Even their half-arsed efforts were superior to most people's finest! There are weak links, but I wouldn't be without them, they all throw some light on the band. Maybe I could live without *Dig It*. I thought McCartney was entitled to have another go at the album (through *Let It Be Naked*) since he was cut out of the original process, but the *Love Album* sounded pointless to me. I'm all for Anthology-type releases, which add to our understanding of the original group as a creative unit, but re-mixes are gilding the lily.

In general, the great thing I admire in The Beatles is the way they were consistently great, even as their styles changed so dramatically. I like the naive young love songs of the early days, the mystical druggy stuff of 1967 and the mix of raw hard rock and studio gloss you get in the last recordings they did. Happiness and a sense of rightness are the essential virtues of their music. The songs are nearly all optimistic, and the sadder ones are consoling. Only a couple sound cynical or defeated. The Beatles were all young men and the hopefulness of youth is captured in that music. The songs obey the timeless musical laws of harmony, order, progression and resolution, which is how we subconsciously want the universe to be. Of course, the music is very beautiful, and, again subconsciously, we tend to believe that what is beautiful is spiritually true.’

PAUL DU NOYER (Journalist, author and founder of *Mojo* magazine) - 2008

'My relationship with The Beatles began on January 25th 1961. I had just opened a club in Liverpool called The Cassanova Club and was looking to book some bands. They had just returned from Hamburg. Stu was still the bass player and Pete was the drummer. As I watched them that night I was struck by their charisma. They weren't conventional rockers, they were more "studenty", more avant-garde. Pete was a very good drummer, very powerful, but the problem was that he was an introvert. Ringo was a clown, he was a Beatle before he became one, but I still maintain that it was Pete who put the beat into The Beatles. He was technically as good as Ringo, if not better. I went into their dressing room after the show and told them that they would be as big as Elvis. Brian Epstein is often quoted as having said that, and he may well have done, but it was me that said it first! John looked at Paul and said: "We've got a right nutter here", but Paul knew who I was and assured John that I had some work for them. I did. I gave them ten bookings there and then. They played their first show for me on February 9th 1961. Three years to that very day, they made their famous appearance on *The Ed Sullivan Show* in America. How's that for progress!

I first heard *Abbey Road* at a friend's house, where *Come Together* was an instant favourite. I listened to it five times in a row – what a great rock 'n' roll song. I also love *Oh Darling!* and *Golden Slumbers*, which is the kind of romantic ballad I would like to hear Paul go back to writing. I really can't understand why he wrote *Maxwell's Silver Hammer* though. He probably doesn't know himself. It relates to a true story and I don't like it at all. I'm not keen on *Octopus's Garden* either; it's a bit soft that one. Overall, I think it's George that comes out best. Being so shy, he'd been overshadowed by John and Paul for all those years. I don't think it was ever done intentionally, but with John and Paul being so powerful he kind of got forced into a subservient role. *Something* and *Here Comes The Sun* showed everyone how good he was. After that he went on to have the first number one as a solo Beatle. I bet that pleased him. Free at last!'

SAM LEACH (Former Beatles promoter) - 2009

‘George Harrison was in my mum's class at school and, as a result, they were good friends. When The Beatles went to Hamburg for the second time, George asked my dad if he would be their driver. My dad asked his dad, and him being a staunch Italian Catholic, of course, said: "You want to go to Germany? With a rock 'n' roll group? No way!" So The Beatles gave the job to Neil Aspinall instead. When I later got to work with Paul on the *War Child* album, I asked him if he remembered David Minchella from the early days. He said that he did, but I'm not sure if that's entirely true. It was nice of him to say so anyway. Because of his association with my mum, I have always had a soft spot for George. I think *Abbey Road* shows him come out as a great songwriter. *Something* has to be one of the best songs ever, by anyone, and the bassline that Paul played on it really inspired me too. I don't actually play that much Beatles stuff any more. I know it all so well that there's really no need to, but if I'm out and one of their songs comes on it's still a nice surprise. The only niggle I have about them is that because of their status, they seem to be immune to the sort of criticism that other bands would receive. I think a lot of the *Sergeant Pepper* album is shit, but because they're The Beatles it doesn't seem acceptable to say that.’

DAMON MINCHELLA (Ocean Colour Scene) - 2007

‛*Abbey Road* is the first Beatles album – along with *Revolver* – that I gave my full attention to, having grown up with their music in the background of my childhood. I can't remember exactly the first time I heard it, but it reminds me of the late eighties and living in Brighton, always with the image of the LP cover. At that time, I was buying up second-hand vinyl records and getting into a lot of sixties and seventies music. Chart music was generally rubbish then. It's tough to pick just one favourite song from the album – *Come Together, Something, Here Comes the Sun* or *Because*. I can't choose. *I Want You (She's So Heavy)* is a track that drew me in. John Lennon's vocal performance, Billy Preston's organ work, the drum fills, the Moog sounds, the stacked arpeggio guitars, and the final cut off at the end. They blew my teenage mind. I could also mention the chords and vocal performance of *Because*, the guitar solo of *Something*, and the strange Moog in *Maxwell's Silver Hammer*. There are some songs that I find less satisfying, mainly Paul's *Maxwell's Silver Hammer, She Came in Through the Bathroom Window* and *Golden Slumbers*. Having said that, they're all strong melodically; great arrangements, the production is inspired and the album wouldn't be balanced without them.

Sometimes I can get Beatles fatigue, especially listening to the early albums. I don't listen to any of them often any more as I've absorbed them into my psyche. However, when I do, I'm always struck by how good they were as a band. George is my favourite for being so understated and laid back. He's pretty good on guitar too! Supergrass were definitely influenced by them, as were 90% of all other guitar bands since. From *Abbey Road* alone, we took influence from the use of the Moog synthesiser, the beautiful, close backing harmonies and the cut off at the end of *I Want You (She's So Heavy)*, which inspired the end of our track *In It For the Money*.

Not only were they fantastic musicians and songwriters, but they were at the right place at the right time. They encapsulated people's hopes and dreams during the beginning of the sixties and developed and progressed with their audience through the decade. They're still relevant today because their songs stand up so well, the production is truly ingenious and they've carved their own space in the public consciousness. ⟩

MICK QUINN (Supergrass) – 2011

❛Most people's favourite Beatles albums are usually ones like *Revolver* or the *White Album*, so when I was eleven or twelve I went for *Abbey Road* as a bit of a stubborn thing, to be like nah, I don't like them ones, but of course I like all of them! I love the front cover and of course that zebra crossing is really iconic. I've recorded at Abbey Road studios and also did a rehearsal with Burt Bacharach there for the Electric Proms. When I did my stuff I was in a little vocal booth, but with Burt Bacharach we were in the main room (Studio 2) that The Beatles recorded in. Most of it is original, there's still the same piano and stuff like that. You could really hear, I mean obviously it's your imagination, but if you sit there in silence and concentrate hard enough, you could really hear the amazing tunes that The Beatles wrote, echoing off the walls. You could imagine them at the piano and arguing in the control room. You could just feel it.

I've always rated Paul McCartney as one of my favourite singers, and the fact that he can sing and play bass the way he does is quite mesmerising. His voice on *Oh! Darling* is ridiculous. It's incredibly hard. Have you ever tried to sing along and get roughly the same tones as he does on that song? Going from sounding like Ozzy Osbourne to sounding like Joni Mitchell is pretty incredible. He's definitely my favourite vocalist from the group because he's a bit more soulful, that's more my kind of thing, but on the anniversary of John Lennon's death we were in Paris and I couldn't sleep, so I turned on the TV and watched a performance from when he was with Yoko. He had so much charisma on stage. He seemed really tortured, but still 100% content with himself. I do love his voice and stuff, but Paul's is more right up my street. I would love to cover a Beatles song, I mean, of course, there are hundreds to choose from, but I think you have to be careful because there aren't many that you can better. I think when you cover a song it's important that you can either do a different version that people really connect to, like they did with the original, or a better version that crosses over. The Beatles were completely adventurous to the point of being fearless, which is rare even now, let alone way back then.❜

ADELE (Solo artiste) – 2011

‘The Beatles were a collection of four individual talents, each of whom could easily have found success in their own right. Their personalities and sense of humour played a very important part in making them accessible to the public, and between them they produced such a mass of songs that it makes it very hard to pick out favourites.

I bought an original copy of their first album, *Please Please Me*, and my interest extends to the *Love* album, which I listened to whilst travelling through the Lake District today. It might not be a Beatles album in the traditional sense, but I think it's a fabulous celebration of their music. All the original recordings are still there. From their more conventional albums, *Abbey Road* has a very good feel to it. Highlights for me would be *Something, You Never Give Me Your Money* and *Because*.’

ROB BRYDON (Actor and comedian) – 2009

‘*Abbey Road* conjures up magic and the imagination of early childhood, which is poetically expressed through songs such as *Octopus's Garden* and *Maxwell's Silver Hammer*. My other favourites include *She's So Heavy* and *Polythene Pam*, although there's nothing I'd leave out. It's the perfect album. Their songs had a certain something which is very rare, they generated human experience. Their music found a common thread in consciousness, coming straight from Liverpool and awakening generation after generation worldwide. It's what every artiste dreams of. If a song like *I Am The Walrus* came out tomorrow, people's heads would explode, but you've got to remember that that song is over forty years old! I would love to be able to create music as mind bending and far out as that. If I could create a song that still had that kind of impact after forty something years, I would feel pretty accomplished. They took pop music, twisted it all round and then tied it up in a bow.’

❛When I was 14, my friend Tommy invited me to go to The Cavern Club. I'd seen rock 'n' roll in a theatre environment with Cliff and The Shadows, but the idea of seeing music in a small club seemed appealing. I can still remember the atmosphere, the smell of cheap perfume and disinfectant. That night there were five bands on. We planned to leave before the end to avoid getting into trouble, but that was before we caught sight of the spacemen, well they may as well have been. Yes, it was The Beatles! They looked like nothing we'd ever seen before. All the other bands had quiffs and Fender Strat guitars, but here were these strange lads with brushed forward hair and Rickenbacker guitars. When they opened the set with *Some Other Guy*, well, there was nobody to touch them. Don't believe anyone who says The Rolling Stones were the real bad lad rockers, it's rubbish! Before The Beatles got into suits they were absolutely untouchable.

My album choice comes from the end of that decade. I'm not one of these cultist people who feel they have to choose one of the more hip albums like *Revolver* or *The White Album*. I'm quite happy to pick a more mainstream recording, which is *Abbey Road*. My wife and I had just got married and moved into a huge eighteen-room Victorian house. Some of our friends moved in as lodgers and *Abbey Road* was never off the turntable. It provided the soundtrack to our lives that year. Lyrically, I love *She Came In Through The Bathroom Window* and *You Never Give Me Your Money*, but, above all, I have chosen it for the masterpiece that is *The End*, which never fails to drive me to tears. The poignancy of that song is immense, especially when you consider that it was the final song on their final album. What a beautiful piece of writing, what a statement.

Years later, I saw grainy black and white footage of the boys performing *Some Other Guy* in The Cavern. I had tears streaming down my face as I watched it. I realised I had witnessed history. There are very few people that can truly be described as genius. Occasionally people will come along and move the artistic furniture around, which is perfectly fine, but then you get the likes of Picasso, Oscar Wilde, Elvis, Bob Dylan and The Beatles who all invented completely new furniture. They changed the landscape for ever.❜

WILLY RUSSELL (Writer and composer) - 2006

LET ME INTRODUCE YOU TO...
...THE ACTS YOU'VE KNOWN FOR ALL THESE YEARS

ADELE (Solo artiste)

ANDRÉ BARREAU (The Bootleg Beatles)

ANDY McCLUSKEY (OMD)

ASTRID KIRCHHERR (Beatles' photographer and friend)

BARRIE CADOGAN (Touring musician - Morrissey and Primal Scream)

BEN GRUBIN (Hockey)

BENJAMIN ZEPHANIAH (Poet)

BILL WYMAN (The Rolling Stones)

CHARLIE REID (The Proclaimers)

CHAS HODGES & DAVE PEACOCK (Chas & Dave)

CHRIS O'NEILL (George Harrison in the film Backbeat)

COLIN BLUNSTONE (The Zombies)

CRAIG REID (The Proclaimers)

DAMON MINCHELLA (Ocean Colour Scene)

DAN GOLD (Celebrity tattoo artist)

DARRIN MOONEY (Primal Scream)

DAVE McCABE (The Zutons)

DONOVAN (Solo artiste)

EDDY GRANT (Solo artiste)

EDWINA CURRIE (Former Member of Parliament)

SIR ELTON JOHN (Solo artiste)

GARY MOORE (Thin Lizzy and solo artiste)

GLENN HUGHES (Deep Purple and Black Country Communion)

GRAHAM COXON (Blur and solo artiste)

HERBERT HOWE (Celebrity hairdresser)

IAN McLAGAN (The Small Faces and The Faces)

JAMES MAY (TV presenter)

JAMES WALSH (Starsailor)

JAYNE TORVILL & CHRISTOPHER DEAN (Olympic figure skating gold medallists)

JERM REYNOLDS (Hockey)

JOE BONAMASSA (Black Country Communion and solo artiste)

JOHN GORMAN (The Scaffold)

KEN DODD (Comedian)

KLAUS VOORMANN (Designer of the Revolver sleeve and Beatles' friend)

LEMMY (Motörhead)

LES DENNIS (Actor and comedian)

LESLIE WOODHEAD (Documentary Film-maker – first to film The Beatles)

MATHEW HORNE (Actor – Gavin & Stacey, The Catherine Tate Show)

MICK QUINN (Supergrass)

NICK ACKERMAN (The Virgins)

OLI BROWN (Solo artiste)

PAUL DU NOYER (Journalist, author and founder of Mojo magazine)

PETER DOHERTY (The Libertines, Babyshambles and solo artiste)

SIR RANULPH FIENNES (Adventurer)

RICHIE HAVENS (Solo artiste)

RICKY HATTON (Former world champion boxer)

ROB BRYDON (Actor and comedian)

ROBERT WHITAKER (Beatles' official photographer)

SAM LEACH (Early Beatles' promoter)

SIMON FOWLER (Ocean Colour Scene)

SPENCER LEIGH (Merseybeat historian, author and radio presenter)

STAN BOARDMAN (Comedian)

STEPHEN GRAHAM (Actor – Snatch, Gangs of New York, This Is England)

STEVEN ADLER (Guns 'N' Roses)

STEVIE RIKS (Impressionist)

STOK (Graffiti artist)

THE BANGLES (Musicians)

THE LOST BROTHERS (Musicians)

TIM BURGESS (The Charlatans)

VICTOR SPINETTI (Actor - A Hard Day's Night, Help! and Magical Mystery Tour)

WALTER TROUT (Solo artiste)

WILLY RUSSELL (Writer and composer – Educating Rita, Shirley Valentine, Blood Brothers)